The "I" of a Woman

How to Succeed in Life With Humor and Grace

Dragonstone Press
2018

Dedication

*I am blessed to have so many wonderful women
as my friends—especially members of Women of Words (WOW)
writers group—who are supportive, smart, and kind.*

Acknowledgment

I want to thank my writing friends and other women who have reviewed
my words and given me insightful and sound advice.

Especially I want to thank Sue Stein, who took my many words and ways of showing
them, added graphics, and brought the book to life, from the cover to the back page.

The Why Behind *The "I" of a Woman*

Women, I am told, on the average speak two to three times as many words a day than men do. So when he is done talking, she still has a lot left to say. That's why we have girlfriends!

The "I" of a Woman is full of the ideas and feelings women in general believe/don't believe, feel/pretend about, ignore/deal with, rejoice or whine about. You get the idea. It's what we share with our best friends.

I hope you react as you read these pages—with joy, with recognition and acknowledgment, or even with sadness. I watched my "test market" of girlfriends react to the book, sometimes with a big smile, others a flash of emotion I didn't recognize. Mostly I want you to know that YOU are not alone in your reactions. Your women friends around the world are with you.

I am a writer and use words to connect and tell a story. These are my words. Certainly not all are my life stories—in fact, very few are, but they belong to someone—maybe you.

Women need to listen to and support other women as we journey through life "with humor and grace."

I'd love to hear your reactions.

Connie Anderson

NOTE:
Author's revised
contact email is
Connie@WordsandDeedsInc.com

Little Girls

Little girls play at being big girls long before they need to.

They scold, pamper, and feed their well-dressed babies. If their doll messes, they change its diaper. They gossip over tea and cookies. And at the end of play, they put everything in its place—like they are.

They know exactly what to say to each other and to their dolls, because they've heard us say it.

Quickly each one acts out her own mother's day—and that of her mother before her—being loving and caring for her children, her home, and her husband.

Little Boys

When little boys play, 10 bad guys are shot dead, 14 troublemakers are karate chopped into oblivion—and someone will win while others will lose.

Later the space under the table becomes a track for roaring racecars that circle and circle.

They play loudly and with vigor, and put their toys away only if prodded.

The boys play and play—but never play at being a father. Quickly each acts out his father's day—and that of his father before him—working, working, working.

I am an "unwilling" single again; chocolate and ice cream help to take the pain away. This also means that no one can get into my pants—not even me.

Every time I walk into a singles bar I can hear Mom's wise words:
"Don't pick that up—you don't know where it's been!"

Marriage changes passion. Suddenly you're in bed with a relative.

I wore white
to all *my* weddings.

Wouldn't you know it...
Brain cells come and brain cells go,
but FAT cells live forever.

He said, "Go ahead...
cross the line"—
and I took a joyful leap.

What a joy to discover a wonderful new author, and share
those books with your mother or sister or daughter.

If I'd seen this coming sooner,
I would have ducked or hid.

The difference
between "Yes" and "No"
can be very subtle—
and it can depend on whether
you are hearing it—or saying it.

His insincerity was,
well…

Men all have something wrong with them.
Why can't they be perfect like us?

At times do you get tired
of listening or pretending
you're interested in what he's saying?

When my friend urged me to sign up
for an exercise class, I was told to wear
comfortable clothing. If I had any
loose-fitting clothing, I would not have
joined a club.

Confession: You can eat cheesecake
right out of the freezer.

Blindsided

As we get older
we all want more—
more friends, new and long-time,
more thank yous going out than coming in,
more I Love You notes,
more forgiveness given and received,
more quiet and joyful time with family,
and more long walks.

We need to say "Yes" and "No" more,
because both are beautiful words
when said at the right time.

Some days getting older comes
at me like a bullet train—
and other days I feel
like I'll live forever.
I negotiate with my body
to keep it on my side,
so I can live life fully engaged—
and not as an old fool.

ZZZZZZ

My husband of many years was sleeping soundly, and snoring loudly.

I could have poked him to stop.
I could have insisted he see a doctor
I could have slept on the sofa.

No, I stayed there, next to him, listening, filled with extreme gratitude that
he was still here with me, healthy and happy. ZZzZZZZzzz

Some of Us

Some of us drink,
And some of us make others drink.
Some of us write,
Others are ingredients for a writer's stew.
Some of us are thirteen,
While others act like they are *still* thirteen.
Some of us collect things,
Others collect friends.
Some of us are often overwhelmed,
While others have daily peace.
Some of us enjoy lightning bolts,
And others prefer lightning bugs.
Some of us make shoot-from-the-hip plans,
And others always have a Plan B.

Plan A
Plan B

Life isn't long enough for some
of us dreamers—
and others never start to live
their dreams.

When a never-married man says
you look older than he does, you
can't help that he looks 25. He
should try raising three kids alone,
now all teenagers.

Women who whine give negotiating
a bad name.

It's scary when you and your
daughter are both dating—
and she gives you advice.

I believe the note section of a smartphone has its place when dating. What outfit did I wear? What did we talk about? Where did we go?

Remember...if the world didn't suck, we'd all fall off.

You can't undo some things.

When I'm on a date and a hot flash strikes, I feel like a dog that wants to stick its head out the car window.

Magic Mirror

"Mirror, mirror, on the wall, who's the fairest of them all?"

"Jeez, woman. Is it always up to me? Do you need me
to say you're beautiful so you will believe it?"

"But mirror, you always say the right thing."

"Woman, get a grip. You're in charge of how
you feel. You've got to BELIEVE!"

"Mirror, mirror, do I need a facelift?"

A plastic surgeon's business card dropped from the mirror's magic frame.
The image shrugged, "Sorry…I get a little commission."

I'm a good custodian of the earth:
I recycle newspapers, cans, glass—and men.

Don't let your life become a sad,
sappy country-western song.

 Yes, the grass may be greener over
there, but it still needs mowing.

It can be so cleansing to eliminate the negative
people from your life—so do it NOW!

Wedding Day

The "Wedding March" floated down the aisle. When it reached the back of the church, my eyes filled with tears of joy.

The man of my dreams and my heart beamed at me as he waited patiently up front with the rest of the wedding party.

My mom walked me down the aisle and gave my hand to Tom in marriage.

At that moment, I felt my long-gone dad take his firm hands off my shoulders.

It's important not to yield to gossip, by repeating it, making it up, or believing it.

Laugh early and laugh often.

Put the "self" in reliance.

With some training, I can become the editor of my feelings...and my life.

You are important. Now believe it!

Play the cards you're dealt, especially the joker.

Stories

My once-husband has taken up residence in my head again.

When we were married we didn't dance around the truth—because in our relationship there was never any music playing—ever.

When I am lonely, I forget about all his lies; he was a very good liar after years of practice.

But sometimes I can only remember the good times and even today, I look the other way rather than face the truth.

If I were honest with myself, I'd admit that I've left out "the real story" once again.

The yellow brick road has potholes,
hills, and needs better signs.

When you sabotage yourself,
it can mean "maybe never
ever" will you be happy.

After the movie
starts, a phone rings,
and everyone glares—
but nobody answers.

Much of life is a crapshoot.
Go ahead and roll 'em.

Mirrors and cameras almost never lie,
but usually show the truth.

THE COVER

Somehow this man and woman had found each other.

He smiled and she frowned.
She sat stiffly and he slouched.
He told dirty jokes but she didn't laugh.
He was scruffy and she perfectly groomed.
He was smart and she played dumb.
She loved her family; he didn't like his.
He loved loud music—and she didn't.
She is high strung and he's laid back.
She loved him, and he loved her back.

There is a cover for every kettle.

When I looked out and saw the world...I pulled the shades.

I never want to be on the committee of self-important do-gooders.

Met a new man, and he's a broken piece of perfect.

When I was the groom's mother, I was told in certain words: Show up. Shut up. Wear beige.

 Give life your best shot, and when it's time, go out with a bang.

Sorry

Sometimes when I answered the phone, a hang-up would make me suspicious.
Other times, it was my husband saying, "Have to work late," which added to my concern.

I accidentally discovered meal and motel receipts
in his pockets for places I've never been.

He is ratted out by the perfume on his clothes,
an overpowering scent that I wouldn't wear.

I've caught him—and when I show him proof, he says, "I'm so sorry."

He always says he's sorry. Is he sorry he cheated—or sorry he got caught?

Now what?

They were like chess players dropped
into a Ping-Pong match—
they didn't know what they were doing,
but together they stayed,
and played to win at life.

Taking care of yourself might be
a warm and luxurious bath after a long
and stressful day.

It's not IF,
but WHEN.

You cannot put a price on watching a child
sleeping peacefully, especially your own.

Yes, sometimes a good cry is healthy, even though it ruins your mascara.

To better days, better nights, and better choices.

His commitment to me is as predictable as a sunset—and just as heartwarming.

Give yourself the gift of forgiving THEM!

You are never too old to have your mother ask, "You did WHAT?"

Life Partners

He started drinking to protect himself against
all the "ifs," "ands," and "buts" staggering his life.

She started lying to reduce the number
of times the spoken word hurt her soul too much.

He started holding his breath for long periods
to focus on anything else but the journey
that illness has forced upon him.

She started wearing a mask of pretend annoyance
to dissuade people from asking her, "Why?"

When he and she started measuring themselves
against others who battle life—they realized they were
the most important persons in each other's life.

It Takes Two

We were married—at least I was.

He was the kind of guy I didn't really trust to go out for cigarettes
and return the same night to our revolving-door life.

We never really saw eye-to-eye on what being married meant,
and I wasn't a happy member of that club.

I felt like I was doing a ventriloquist act, hoping he'd say what I wanted to hear.

My "life-sucks" file was bulging from daily entries—and nothing good
ever started with him saying, "You can trust me."

And then, things got worse, as they always seem to do...

Living the plaintive words of a country-western song, our tunes were so different,
until one day I turned his music off and said goodbye.

DREAMS

Husband, who, I wonder, has custody of your brain? I know that actually thinking things through takes time, but you seem to have more time than energy, commitment, or desire.

I have many ideas lolling around in my brain, and these ideas, still unfulfilled, are like a mean dog nipping at my heels, reminding me to take it out for a walk into the world to see who it might bite.

Unlike you, I no longer want to sit on the moral fence. Falling off either way is better than simply sitting.

Girlfriends

"Betsy, want to go shopping Saturday?"

"Angie, want to go to lunch Friday?"

"Dana, want to go for a long walk today?"

"Susan, want to have a good visit over coffee at ten?"

"Katherine, want to go antiquing at our favorite place?"

"Diane, want to go to the bookstore and then have tea?"

A woman has a lot of friends and spreads them out across her life. And for me, each one has her "special place" in my life, and in all truth, I can say, "Of all my friends, today I love YOU the best!"

Are you strong and committed enough *to try until you get it right?*

At times it is a challenge to say, "I'm sorry," and mean it.

Progress is to take one step forward without taking two steps back.

It's a good day when you are expecting something special to happen—and it does.

Never attempt to reform a man—particularly a husband, especially if he's yours.

In the right hands, words of truth can push through a crapload of lies.

If you were/are married to a narcissist, you'd know he always had to be the hero of his own story. Same is true of narcissist girlfriends. In either case, it gets old after a while. You have to start somewhere...and it is easier to "divorce" a girlfriend than a husband.

Humor is a wonderful tool—unless it is used to demean and make fun of someone.

It's not easy to outrun your demons, especially in five-inch stilettos.

I Am Not Doing "Nothing"

Here I am, sleeping and crying and doing nothing day after day, wallowing in my new status as "a widow."

As I listen to the phone ring and ring, I think about answering, but right now I can't. I hope they leave a message.

Opening my puffy eyes, I drag my unwilling self to the kitchen to eat cold leftover sausage pizza and drink yesterday's horrible-tasting coffee.

I peer out to watch the world go by, and then glance at the pile of mail, the dozens of unopened sympathy cards.

I am not doing "nothing."
I am surviving.
I am grieving.
I am…Alone.

He had always been in charge of pushing my buttons, pulling my strings, and controlling my words. It's a new day, and I'm no longer a puppet, waiting on his demands.

Life, like medicine,
doesn't always taste
good going down.

Joyful or sad? Your tears
taste the same.

Every day you need some deep
you-to-you talk so you can learn
how to ration hope...and love.

Good-bye

Our relationship was wonderful, and I was so happy.

He called often, as expected.
He came over, as promised.
He brought wonderful gifts.
He carried in great meals for our special time together.

He became the center of my life,
a reason to wait for the phone to ring.
And ring it did one evening
as I watched for him out the window.

"Ann, it's me. My wife said I cannot see you anymore. I'm sorry.
Good-bye."

He's sorry?

In life and in love, it's important to know when to cut your losses.

What is more powerful than the silence after her sigh when your friend admits, "I know!" (Sighhhhh!)

In the "getting-to-know-you" phase of a relationship, if he's still talking about his high school feats when the first date is over—and he doesn't know what you do for a living—he just might be a bit too self-centered even for a desperate woman.

Women have to learn to simply say "thank you" sometimes.

We can't always explain why we do something for a man. You can think of all the reasons, but they don't sound the same out loud.

If I "ate my feelings" every day, I'd be huge.

For most women, when a man says he "wants to watch" when you undress, remember, he might actually mean "the TV."

Dating

Smiling absently, my blind date continued,
"I blah, blah, blah."

After taking a deep breath and,
without looking up from his food,
he droned on about himself,
"Blah, blah, blah, blah, blah, blah."

It's hard for me to have a two-way conversation
when I am the last thing on his mind.

Truth be told, he doesn't need a date.
He needs a bigger mirror
for he already has a very
meaningful relationship
with himself.

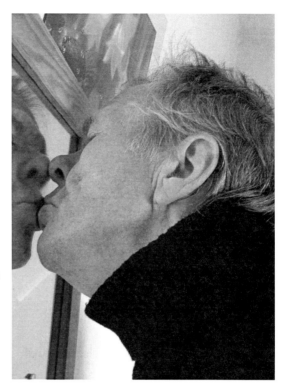

If it's time to draw a firm line in the sand, make sure it's not quicksand.

"Widow," it said, so I didn't apply. I don't ever want the job.

For some, a penny for your thoughts is wildly overspending.

The truth: Sometimes it's an unexpected distraction.

Don't ever give anyone the power to break your heart.

For Me?

The florist's familiar blue delivery truck drove past my house and down the street.
Oh, well, maybe next time.

When the doorbell rang, I opened the door. There was the florist delivery guy holding
a huge arrangement of my favorite red roses—a whole dozen.

Sweetly I asked, "Are those lovely flowers
for me?" as I wondered who sent them.

"No ma'am, your neighbor isn't home.
May I please leave these with you?"

Some days you get what you deserve,
but other days you don't

Heck, I'll buy *myself* flowers.

Some days it is hard, while some days it is easy to be grateful for all you have.

Have you yelled at someone recently, and it was not about that person? Stuffing painful emotions means that they have to come out in unpleasant ways, and they do—including illness.

You can't deny that the importance of "perfection" is an ugly myth.

He told me that he loved me. I believed it, before I learned that he has always been a liar, practicing daily.

Letting Go

I love much about our big empty nest. I can get $20 from an ATM machine, and it stays in my wallet for a week. When it's gone, I am the one who spent it.

I can clean the house and it says clean—mostly.

I love the quiet, but miss the noise. I love the cleanliness but miss seeing their shoes at the door.

I have let go of them, but hold the memories near and dear.

Gotta go, I think I hear someone calling, "Mom."

Rats, it was just blaring from the TV, not my kids.

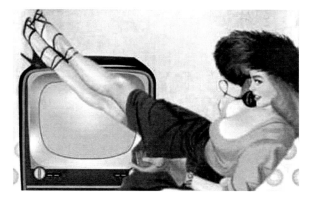

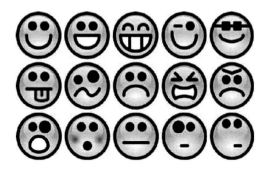

When you are in emotional pain and someone asks, "How are you?" do you tend to say, "Fine!" Starting now, be honest with yourself and others. Feel those emotions because until you acknowledge them, you cannot start to heal them.

It isn't always bad news when someone says, "We need to TALK."

Some days we have to admit that our words are very cruel weapons.

Ranting and raging against another person's flaws is the definition of futility.

Your body and soul have been waiting for you to reclaim yourself, deciding that you are strong and that the broken parts are healing. Embrace those emotions and pay attention to them.

Going forward, you must accept that he is never going to change—and neither are you.

When your aging mother wants to pay for something like a meal, or gives you money for a gift, let her do it. If you don't, you are insulting her and making her feel useless and without value.

Unringing a Bell

Today I really do not want to hear from friends,
women who are
     sometimes being foolish,
     sometimes being gullible,
     sometimes being stupid.

A ringing phone doesn't always have to be answered,
But most often I do.
Quickly the caller's problem snakes
along the phone line into my unwilling ear—
and absorbs my life, stealing my time.

"Do you know what my husband just did?"
"I think I met 'the one.'"
"Our daughter is dating a jerk."

I listen, I advise, I suggest.
I polish my nails, clean out drawers
and on and on,
I listen, I advise, I suggest some more.

I really don't charge enough.

Listen up. Here's the truth.
Now believe it.

Parent alert: When you visit your child at camp and he misses you—make sure it is enough to make you feel good, but not enough to make him want to come home early.

She knew. They all knew.
No one cared,
but they should have.

I love to tap my fingers on the keys to create my life for real, and on the page.

We all try to keep secrets, even when they're awesome... but some days we don't.

Rated "The Best"

She said:

You're my best friend. You listen, are compassionate and empathetic.

You pretend I don't have faults, but slap me with your powerful words if I deserve it.

You are there when I really need you—and also on ordinary days.

We've shared sad and happy times, crazy-making divorces, the joyous birth of grandchildren—and ideas. Oh what wonderful daydreams we've shared for the future.

You are the best!

I said:

I am simply happy to be nominated.

If you look out and see rain or snow or strong winds, you are still alive—still "above ground"— so do the things you've been resisting because it could be now or never.

Super heroes abound on TV, in books, and movies. I see mine every morning in the mirror. I don't need rescuing; I can rescue myself.

Dear God, please listen now. I'm talking to you.

When I got close, he didn't, so I got closer, but he then moved away.

Everyone

"Honey, you need to make a to-do list, and then get stuff done so you can cross it off."

"Honey, it feels great to get organized and accomplish things."

"Honey, did you remember to wash the clothes you're taking along?"

"Mom, leave me alone," the twenty-something daughter said.

"Honey, you are the most disorganized person in the world," I said knowingly.

"Mom, you obviously don't know EVERYONE."

Enough said.

He said he wanted to move in with me, and that he would get me a ring. He moved in, but the only ring I got was the one around the bathtub that he left for me to clean up. He did that only once... before I helped him move on.

A woman called. I learned that my husband is unfaithful to two women.

Next time I'll say
"Yes" to taking
care of *me*.
Then I'll be safe.

Get aboard. Life's a one-way trip, so do something good.

Fur Envy

A tall, beautiful woman and I walked out of the mall together.

Wrapped in a street-length faux-fur, she looked spectacular.

Every inch of my five-foot shortness was consumed with jealousy.
Fur-wrapped, I looked like a wooly-bear caterpillar—
or a sumo wrestler.

I had to say it. "You look wonderful in that coat.
In my next life, I want to be tall."

Smiling she replied, "Yes, but don't do it in junior high
unless you really want to play sports where tall girls rule."

Standing Inspection

My know-it-all mother-in-law was coming over to see her new grandchild.

As a first-time mom, I tried exhaling slowly to control my panic. True to the old saying, I was like a duck on a lake, calm on the surface and paddling like crazy underneath.

The clock raced around quickly to her arrival time.

She came. I watched as she cooed and played—and the baby smiled his way into her heart, and she into mine.

We passed each other's inspection.

Now I understand that we two women have a very special bond… and why.

It's hard not to see divorce as "a failure." Change your perspective. Divorce opens you to new worlds, opportunities, and people. Go forward with knowledge that you will survive and—after a while—thrive.

You can't have it all—
but you can and really
should enjoy what
you do have.

Some days I just want
to sit down and have
a cigarette—and I don't
even smoke.

Help me down because my
ivory tower is tottering.
Catch me, please.

All I Want To Be ...

When I was little, I wanted
to be a singer and sing my
father's favorite songs.

When I graduated high school,
I wanted to study to be a teacher,
but taking chemistry scared me.

When I became an adult, I wanted
to have a talk show because
I had a lot to say.

When I grew older, I wanted to
write a book because people said
I was funny.

When I...after I...while I...before it's too late—don't let me talk myself out of my
dreams.

I need to pick one—*and do it for me!*

For him, she's the path of least resistance.

Red Ferrari for Sale—
Husband moved on; car
also needs to go. Write
check to the wife.

I did a trustworthy
"smell test."
He stinks.

Sticky Notes—colorful
reminders when your
memory fails.

If you don't have the ability to
see humor in chaos—get it!

My Favorite Song

The song I love most makes me happy.
The song I love most makes me sad.

The song I love most makes me remember my mother.
The song I love most makes me want to dance.

The song I love most makes me feel patriotic.
The song I love most takes me back to high school.

The song I love most is one that
Makes me feel something—in that moment.

Define your own success
because the choices are
yours, and it is your life.

One cannot always love and be wise—
but one can try.

I am quitting smoking—
again, but this is
the last time.

Give yourself permission to yield
to inertia. Being inactive isn't a
sin; at times it's simply a treat.

Life gets better when you finally
understand that the sun
will come up and shine tomorrow,
and so will you.

Listening

"Honey, I had a great day today."

"Pass the salt, Anne."

"I found the perfect dress for the party."

"Where's the sports page?"

"And guess what, John, I got promoted!"

"Ahhh, haaa."

"I'm talking to you. Are you listening?"

"Yeah, you spent money on a dress you didn't need."

Sadly, I have wasted precious time on him that I'll never get back.

Don't argue with an idiot,
because people watching may
not be able to tell the difference.

If only he looked at me
like…(fill in the blank).

Angry colorblind people
don't "see red."

No one believed in me,
not even me. So sad.

Wait, God. We need to talk.
I'm not ready to go yet.

Life

One day I'm a young woman, dreaming of my ideal future and success.

One day I'm planning my wedding…then so quickly our babies are born.

One day we're sending them off to college for their own fun and education.

One day they dream of their ideal future—and I wonder about my part in it.

One day their father leaves, not for school or work, but for another woman.

One day both of the children have jobs that take them far away, and I'm alone again.

No one told me life would pass by me so swiftly—or was I just not paying attention?

I'm not in the same pond with the other ducks, and never will be.

Fear and anxiety.
Joy and laughter.
A bad day rescued.

You have my heart;
I have someone else's.
Wanna trade?

Some women who are alone, widowed or divorced, decide to leave their long-time friends, home, and church, and move states away to be near family. This makes for a very happy adult child and doted-on grandchildren—and more love from Grandma.

How was Your Day?

The kids arrive home from school.

"Son, how was your day?"

"Fine, Mom, it was school."

"How was your day?" I ask my teenage girl.

"Jodie has new cool shoes. We had a fire drill. Marnie got her long hair cut. Mr. Johnson liked my report, and Mrs. Armor is pregnant."

She then clasped her hands over her mouth as if to keep a secret from falling out. "Guess what, Mom. Jim asked me to the dance, my first dance. Can we please go shopping for a pretty dress?"

Why do I learn everything
the hard way? All lessons
don't have to painful.

I'm working on having an
unexpressed thought.
It's like checking with
your brain before
opening your mouth.

Sometimes there's
value in not getting
what you wish for.

A best friend is truly a
gift you give yourself.

Without a sense of humor…you'll go crazy.

What Happened to Me?

What happened to me?

The trip down to tie my shoes is much harder exercise
than pushing away a fully decked-out brownie sundae.

The tiny type, calling out names and numbers,
sinks into the pages of my phone book,
leaving calls unmade because of tiny-type blindness.

The lists, oh the lists that occupy my life to ensure that I remember.
Now, where is that list?

Margaritas, fajitas, and senoritas. They all rhyme with good times.

I know I am getting older because my mirror tells me, my aches tell me—and little kids tell me (even if their mom tries to hush them).

I have bounced back from the man who told me he didn't like to date women who had more facial hair than he did.

Age has its privileges. I am no longer trying to make a good impression at the store or family reunion—or in front of the full-length mirror.

Talking, sharing, laughing.
Women need each other
at every stage and every age.

My body told me to
"Slow down."
I didn't…
and collapsed.
Now I listen.

Now it's my turn—unwillingly
I leave middle age and
march with both joy and mild
trepidation—towards living
and writing my last chapters
in ink.

It's wonderful to
have someone love
you, just the way
you are.

Taking Care

I don't have a dog because I can hardly take care of me.

I don't have a cat because one self-centered creature in a household is enough.

I even kill plants. It's not that I am mean to plants;
I just forget that something other than me needs a stiff drink
and a little attention now and then.

Maybe I'll take up breeding the dust bunnies under my bed.

Do you have someone who loves you just the way you are?

Encouragement is a gift we give others—and ourselves.

Remember that "average" is as close to the bottom as it is to the top. Don't settle for less than your potential—strive for the best.

Darn, I should have looked twice. Next time, if there is one...

If raising children was supposed to be easy, it never would have started with something called "Labor"!

The Life Script

Where's the perfect how-to book on dating?

Where's the script for newlyweds, negotiating the toilet seat, toothpaste, and money?

Where's the guidebook for when I am alone with my first baby who cries all day and night?

Where's the rulebook for dealing with teenagers who know all your buttons and revel in pushing them?

Where's the plan for growing old the best way possible?

When you write down your sound advice, I want a copy before it's too late.

What is better than a good book, a glass of wine, and a roaring fire—all shared with someone special?

The wonder of life happens when you resolve the impact of infertility, and finally have that longed-for baby.

Never say "never."
This rule is too strict, but often not strict enough.

There is wonder in being in charge of your own destiny.

Success is getting a life you enjoy— and then living it to the fullest.

Friends With Benefits

"Friend with benefits" (FWB) has a 21st century sexual reference to some. Not me.

My FWB is Kathy, who has a sporty convertible for sunny days, or Mary Jo, who has a lake cabin for a weekend away.

Barb has a cozy loft by a fabulous ski resort, and Dana welcomes fleeing-winter Northerners to her warm Southwest home.

In my version of FWB, I don't have to get in bed with anyone. If I want to warm my feet, I have an electric blanket and a warm, forgiving dog.

Call 9-1-1. My life is a disaster.

Met her. Became friends.
Gave myself a great gift.

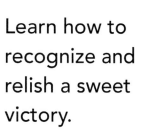

Learn how to
recognize and
relish a sweet
victory.

Always looking backwards
might give you a few insights—
but for sure, will give you
a stiff neck.

Lead with love. Give your
kids a fighting chance.

He was born decent. That's what saved me.

69

Changes

As you age, everything changes. Everything!

Thanks to Mr. Gravity, your boobs drop, sag, and lose
their perkiness.
Your waist broadens—along with your horizons.
Your eyes keep their color, but lose everything else.
Your feet get wide, as do your hips.
You shrink, a little, but it happens.
You need to make your rings bigger as your knuckles swell.

Changes are a fact of life.
We can make them less "noticeable," but they are inevitable.

That's why I like earrings—they always fit!

Revel in the power that
comes from being honest.

Ignore what deserves
to be ignored.

Finally the day comes when
you walk out of the "wrong"
someone's life.
Is it now or soon?

Rejoicing at the magnificence of the
sunrise is better if you can share it.

His lies were good, so good
that even he believed them.

BANKING

I put money in my bank whenever I get some. I take money out by offering my cash card as momentary hostage to an ATM machine.

The ATM's receipt tells me whether I can return again for more take-out— or if the next drive-by must be a deposit.

One day I fear that the hungry machine will not invite me back—or it will, without ceremony, suck up my cash card forever.

That's why I always greet it with a smile and some pleasant small talk.

It's worth the effort to find a good, ethical mechanic who doesn't treat you like an idiot.

After looking and looking, it's wonderful to find a greeting card that says it all.

I had better get a newer map if I am ever going to find the right road for me.

No smart woman should be imprisoned by pride and fear, thinking that she is living her life as a fraud.

We need to work on NOT always being in control.

Battles

Does anyone other than me "do battle"—
with themselves?

I battle with my weight and my craving for chocolate.

I battle with my habit of being messy and disorganized.

I battle with my tendency to talk too much,
and listen too little.

I battle with my kids over mostly unimportant things.

I battle with my boss for more recognition for my work.

Not one of these battles is very important—unless I win, or unless I am good at pretending
I won.

Do you have love letters worth re-reading? If not, write one to yourself.

Sorry, honey, I talk a lot because I'm not good at summarizing.

Evil seeks the helpless, so wear your "in-control" mask.

Have no voice? Then even you can keep a secret.

Choices. Yes, we all have choices, so it's up to you to make the right ones.

FAIR TRIAL

Every day, "Do I look fat in this?" is asked in thousands of marriages.

The husband weighs the value of truth over a white lie. He wants a clean slate as they go to bed tonight, or he knows what will not happen. But instead he blurts out, "Yes, it's too tight."

Seeing her shock, reluctantly he asks, "I'll get a fair trial, won't I?"

Is there a support group for guys who answer without thinking? There should be.

Sometimes the best medicine is having a darn good cry, watching a sappy movie, reading an encouraging letter from someone who loves you— bringing those emotions bubbling up to the surface—and then dealing with them.

One day I wrote a love letter to the past— but then I realized I really didn't want *to go back there.*

Kids are an old goat's joy

A man told me, "You *could be* someone," and I thought: *I already am.*

People Magazine

Waiting at the doctor's office, I started reading this really interesting article in *People* magazine.

They called my name and I got up, magazine in hand.

The doctor (shock of shocks) came in immediately, so I didn't have time to finish reading that article. Later I made my getaway with a colorful year-old gossip magazine stuck in my purse.

I'm embarrassed about what I did, but don't worry, I'll get over it.

Now you are free to open a "window of opportunity."

Women need to accept that divorce can be like an endless pit, only deeper.

Yes, beauty is power...but with time, that power can change hands.

Never let them see you sweat...or even glisten!

What a welcome gift to have a short person sit in front of you at a movie or play.

COMPLAINING

When our partnership called marriage dissolved, I thought
about all the things he did that drove me crazy.

He always put almost-empty milk cartons back into the refrigerator.
He left the family car's gas tank near empty. He used the last stamp.

He did this and that, and it drove me nuts.

However, the week he left, I realized it was me who actually did those things,
and now I have no one else to blame.

How loud, how firm, and how confident are you when you say "No!"?

Stop screaming when the person doesn't value your opinion enough to listen.

At what age were you adult enough to distinguish between "want" and "need"?

Worry is the price for what might happen— but odds are that it usually won't.

Daughter's Boyfriend

"Mom, he's so nice, and we have such fun together."

"Mom, he forgot my birthday."

"Mom, he calls me every day."

"Mom, we get into an argument every time we talk on the phone."

"Mom, we have so much fun, but he's so busy with friends, and work and other things that I hardly ever see him."

I started to wonder: Why does this boyfriend's behavior sound so familiar?
Then I looked at my own life.

"Daughter, are you the only one in this relationship? If he doesn't meet your needs, what do you need him for?"

I need to ask myself the same questions.

This is the day to
dream new dreams.

I'm working on believing the
truth that I can't change others; I
can only change myself.

We need the grace to
know when to listen…
and when to talk. Yes,
everything has to do
with grace.

My new boyfriend is more
of a comfortable sedan
than a sports car.

I'm thinking of starting a club…

Picking Your Man

My mother had the Rule of Five:

"Don't tell me about a new man until after five dates, and don't proclaim him 'the one' until after five months."

I tell her he's a little insensitive and immature, but he has a nice car. I share with her that he and I don't have the same beliefs, but he's fun.

Then she says, "Let this man ripen on the vine before you decide whether to pick him."

Having already tasted too many sour grapes, I now want the right blend in a man.

Finally I listen and I understand…and I can wait.

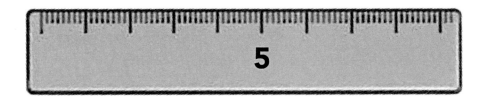

Marriage isn't always permanent—and divorce isn't fatal.

Never put your life on hold for Mr. Right.

Bless the day when you can feel the presence of a Higher Power, as you know it.

A good day ends with not having to cook dinner tonight—or with having someone special to cook with.

Hardware Store

Going to the hardware story with my daddy was at least a two-hour tour because he'd carefully explain what all the fun things were used for. We examined chisels, hammers, penny nails and a measuring tool, all needed to make a birdhouse. And we made one, and watched the baby wrens grow.

Today I go to the hardware store alone. I wander up and down the aisles to touch and hold the same things that I held in my little-girl hands. Thoughts flow over me as I remember, and decide that today I will buy a birdhouse and start new memories.

Thanks, Dad for still whispering advice in my ear and guiding me. I know how to use both my hands and the many wonderful secrets in the hardware store. Lucky me.

A child's laughter is music to everyone's ears.

You can only hope
that your children
will find mates who
won't break their
hearts.

It's true: Life is always
a two-way street.

Watch out so the word "but"
doesn't always get you in trouble.

Disposing of (not recycling) a dead
marriage. Rest in peace (not pieces).

An "Ing" Coming On

Begging, licking, wiggling, wagging, and dancing.

Waiting, tugging, and walking.

Sniffing, looking, greeting, sniffing, walking, and tugging.

Squatting, pooping, and watching.

Smelling, leg lifting, marking, wagging, and tugging.

Resisting, pulling, relenting, and ending.

Entering, drinking, licking, playing, snacking, napping, dreaming.

Napping, dreaming, running, dreaming, and resting.

A dog's life is all about treats, walks, other four-legged friends to sniff, and of course, the humans who love them.

Not a bad way to look at your life: filled with unconditional love, and the desire to make people happy.

More humans should learn from dogs.

He saw a woman wearing a
sweatshirt with "Guess"
on it, so he said "Implants?"
She hit him.

I don't do drugs. I get
the same effect simply
by standing up fast.

I live in my own little world—but it's
okay because they know me here.

I don't approve of political jokes.
I've seen too many of them get elected.

Remarriage

When I heard he was getting remarried, I was very upset. I felt my anger was justified because he had left me for his much younger girlfriend.

And soon, we'll all be together acting as "two happy families" at our son's wedding.

I'll close my eyes to them and be Trent's proud mother. It will be a good day—in spite of our divorce.

We don't always leave the party with the person we used to come with.

A Smart Woman?

Who knows me better than I do?

Then how is it that I make the same dumb mistakes over and over? Don't I ever learn?

Friends stand by me even when I am being stupid. One said, "You're so smart. Why are you with him?"

He lies, cheats, and treats me badly. Well, he's now shown his stripes.

If he was a dog, I'd know he would bite. Why can't I be that smart about men?

That bus doesn't stop here—ever!

His phone rang, and I thought
about answering it,
but didn't even look
at the screen, as tempting
as that was.

Hold him blameless?
No #^&% way!

Dumb move. Your mother
must be so proud.

He owes me a favor. Time to collect before it's too late.

When Will We Learn...

When will we learn...that if a man says something,
we should listen for the truth of it,
and not rewrite his words in our heads.

When will we learn...when he does little-boy things,
and you decide you can and will wait until he grows
up—even though he's already 42.

When will we learn...when he says he doesn't handle
money well, and you loan him some—you won't expect to be repaid.

When will we learn...when he tells the truth as he knows it, that instead of believing,
I can change him, we understand all we can do is accept him.

When will we learn...that believing him would be very bad for us—and telling the truth
is apparently impossible for him.

The storyteller died,
but his stories didn't,
thanks to books.

Plan your journeys. Map joy
and laughter into them.

Yesterday overflowed with sadness.
New day, but same problem.

My mother released her
last breath, ending 47
years of a good marriage.

Celebrating my dad who raised
me, and I turned out just fine.

Remembering

When I remember my mother, I smell her sweet apple pies.

When I remember my grandmother, I smell her fresh cinnamon rolls.

When I remember my favorite aunt, I smell her chewy chocolate chip cookies.

When I think of my father, I can still smell his pipe and his shirt,
sweaty from hard work.

When I think of my mother's garden, the fragrance of June roses fill my senses.

When I think back, it's the loving smells that make the strongest memories.

 See Dick text Jane mindless babbling one-word messages.

Look! Too late…you missed it.

Women know that both listening and talking are not spectator sports.

Being witty isn't always so funny.

Communicating: The willing give-and-take that women friends do so very well, covering a lot of topics and bringing much laughter to every gathering.

A Friend

I have a friend who is newly in love AGAIN, and she's taken up "sighing."
Normally I don't mind sighing, but she is getting to me.

I have a friend who is often unhappy, and she's into complaining a lot.
I can usually work her out of it, but she is wearing me down.

I have a friend who loves to talk, laugh, and share her life stories.
And she listens as much as she talks, making for a real great conversation.

Guess which friend I prefer to spend time with?

Want to Come Over?

"Hello," I answered my cellphone.

"Hi, how are you today?" a woman asked.

"I'm fine."

"Nice, nice day, isn't it?"

"Yes," I answered.

"Is the sun shining there?"

"Yaahhhh."

"May I come over this afternoon?" she asked.

"Maybe."

"Why 'maybe'? Do you have a problem?"

"Yes, I'd like to know who I am talking to first."

"Oops, I dialed the wrong number. My apologies. Nice talking to you."

"But, but…did you still want to come over today?"

When I turned off the TV,
I turned on my brain.

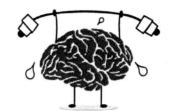

We should always be searching
for the truth...not for someone
to blame.

My judgment
abandoned me.
I sat impotent,
smiling stupidly.

His fire went out. Or, was his love
smothered to death by too many
problems?

Self-sabotage: Completion's really not an option.

The Question

I asked a question there was no answer to, but I asked anyway.
Actually there was an answer, but no one wanted to give it to me.

"Did you know?" I asked.

Lots of throat clearing followed as the women looked at their shuffling feet.
I was trying to be a little smarter about taking care of my heart, but I had to know.

"Did you know?" I repeated. Still no one said anything, and no one made eye contact.

I am a red-eyed amateur at being cheated on and divorced, and didn't know about
the "silence rule," even among best women friends.

Did they know? Did they and didn't tell me? Would they want that to happen to them?
Would they want to know?

All of them knew...and none of them told me. Really pissed me off.

I'm not paranoid. Someone is
watching me, but from above.

She talked while he listened,
most of the time. An almost
perfect married life.

Trust me and lean into me. Oops, too far.
Try again. I'll be there to catch you.

Find your passion.
Act from your heart—
not mine.

Some of the best words
to say—or to hear are:
"I am so proud of you."

Our marriage is slipping
down a gigantic rabbit
hole, with no ladder to
get out.

Sadly, she really
knows firsthand what
"till death us do part"
means.

Some days, the only thing we can do
for someone in pain is to be there,
to listen and to show we care.

When I turn away,
only my back is
facing the problem—
not my heart or my head.

It's hard to compete when you are in love with someone who is in love with someone else.

Don't do the right thing for the wrong reason— or the wrong thing for the right reason.

This is not the time to think about all of the
        Shoulda
        Coulda
        Woulda
in my life.

I should know better.

CHOICES

Sad but true...

We are responsible for all the things we do in our life—
and all the things we don't.

It's a matter of our point of view.